How to be an Effective Chairman

A guide to chairing in small and medium sized organisations

Tom Langdon-Davies FRSA

Dedicated to my Family, who have been Chairmen:

Mary Quicke, my wife
Chairman of the Board of Governors of Queen Elizabeth Community College Crediton
Chairman of the Maize Growers Association
President of the Devon County Show
My daughter Jane
Chairman of Queen Elizabeth College Council
Chairman of Imperial College Ballroom Dancing Society
 My son Mikey
Chairman of Queen Elizabeth College Council
Chairman of Bath University Vegetarian Society

CHAPTERS

PART 1 – WHY?

1. Why have a chairman
2. Why the Organisation needs a chairman
3. What does the chairman do and not do?
4. Digging deeper into the organisation

PART 2 –HOW?

5. How a chairman gets agreement
6. How to find a chairman
7. How to introduce the new chairman into the organisation
8. How can an organisation afford a chairman?
9. How to choose other members
10. Your next step in finding a chairman
11. How a chairman manages meetings
12. Chairing publicly funded community organisations
13. Chairing publicly funded industry organisations
14. Chairing public sector funded charities
15. Chairing joint marketing entities

INTRODUCTION

The role of the chairman is reasonably well documented for large UK businesses, where the separation of roles between chairman and chief executive has become nearly universal.

This guide is an attempt to explain why smaller organisations benefit from having a chairman, and how that chairman should operate. I have used the term "chairman" rather than chair or chairperson to include both sexes. I have used the term "member" to include director, trustee, councillor or any other person sitting on the board or council of a chaired entity.

My underlying assertion is that organisations are more effective with a chairman than without one. Of course a good chairman is better than a bad one, but even a bad one will cause others in an organisation to see the opportunities for improvement more clearly.

It only takes a marginal cumulative effect each year for the value of a chairman to outweigh his costs substantially and in a short amount of time.

Chapter 1

WHY HAVE A CHAIRMAN?

To highlight the long term and statutory commitment of a chairman, I have contrasted what he can do with what can be expected from a freelance mentor:

CHARACTERISTIC	CHAIRMAN	FREELANCE MENTOR
Listens, advises, coaches	Yes	Yes
Supports Chief Executive to perform more effectively	Yes	Yes
Takes on responsibility for developing effective long term strategic thinking	Yes	No
Has a statutory obligation to act in the best interests of the organisation	Yes	No
Has a long term duty to engage with all relevant stakeholders	Yes	No
Is involved in succession planning and board building	Yes	No
Creates long term climate of trust and stability in which the organisation can operate with increased effectiveness	Yes	No

Meetings

Chairing meetings is an art. A good chairman learns how by doing it, sometimes over many years. This enables him to call on a wide range of experience and perspectives when bouncing ideas around with the Chief Executive. It is particularly useful if the CEO's experience is narrowly focussed in a particular sector.

In a quango I chaired, the CEO had been promoted within from an office management position, and although she had previous experience running a small business, it was within the same industry.

As a result of having a large and varied board with wide experience in all aspects of the food and drink industry, as well as other industries and other countries, the CEO was able to engage the organisation in projects outside her previous experience, and to maintain a level of both control and detached vision necessary for their successful outcome.

The CEO has skill gaps

For example the CEO of a charity may have limited commercial experience – it is a good idea for the chairman and some other trustees to have broader experience. The art of using this experience to inform the process of mentoring without cutting across the CEO's authority, or trying to do his job for him, is important.

One charity with which I have worked had a CEO who had only worked in the public sector prior to taking up the job. Fortunately there were several business owners among the trustees, and the chairman had wide experience of advising similar organisations, and had therefore seen many of the possible pitfalls. As a result, the charity was able to engage in many more activities and projects than it would have been able to with a less effective board and chairman.

The core brief of the charity was to manage about two thousand acres of green space in and around a small conurbation. The job could have been done at a basic level by a municipal parks department. However, the aspirations of the charity went far beyond this, and over time it set up

- An educational department that gave inner city children experience of the natural world, including growing and cooking fruit and vegetables.
- A visitors centre with exhibits explaining the habitats under the charity's control

- Several renewable energy projects including biomass boilers, a large photovoltaic array, and a wood processing depot that also supplied fuel to other organisations nearby.
- A shop and restaurant using locally produced food
- A nature reserve of international significance with very rare flora and fauna
- Studios producing and selling handmade crafts to the public
- An annual real ale festival

It is very unlikely that this level of activity would have been achievable without an active and experienced board of trustees supporting and guiding an able and motivated CEO.

Chapter 2

WHY THE ORGANISATION NEEDS A CHAIRMAN

Some organisations are obliged to have one – or would find it very difficult not to.

In UK, charities and Community Interest Companies (CIC's) are legally required to have boards of trustees or directors, and as a result they all tend to have a chairman. This is to ensure that the charitable or community aims of the organisation take precedence over the interests of the managers.

Similarly, in UK and Northern Europe at least, publicly owned companies very rarely have gone for long without a chairman, and are usually required to have one. The situation is different in the US where there is neither a legal nor a customary requirement to separate out the role of chairman from that of chief executive. This is a contentious issue, but many shareholders and academics are of the opinion that in general, businesses operate better when the roles are separated, even in the largest American corporations.

Chapter 3

WHAT DOES THE CHAIRMAN DO AND NOT DO?

According to the Institute of Directors (IOD), one of the main failings of chairmen is to try to do the Chief Executive's job. This is hardly surprising when you consider that many chairmen were previously CEO's of the same company. Nonetheless it is not the job of the chairman, and most CEO's will resent excessive interference in their day-to-day operational management of the organisation.

Leading the Board

A chairman must lead the board. He presides over their meetings, and is responsible for the Agenda, even if the job of writing it is delegated. He is responsible for creating the space in which constructive discussion of all aspects of the organisation's business can take place, and all members can contribute. He will if necessary advise the board on the need to make decisions, but will not consciously seek to manipulate the board to reach a particular conclusion. In practice, though, the board will look to him and the CEO for guidance, and where those two are in agreement, it would be usual but not inevitable for the board to accept the broad direction they suggest.

The qualities required to do this are self-confidence, usually acquired through experience, listening, which can be learned and is all too rare in those who have not been taught how to, and charisma, which arises from being simultaneously in control and open to contribution.

In order to lead the board effectively a chairman must also know his fellow directors and their strengths, so that he can draw them out on relevant matters, or conversely rein them in when they become too long winded. A new chairman is well advised to call each of his fellow members and discuss privately with them their views on the strengths and weaknesses of the organisation, and possible future threats and opportunities.

This can be particularly important with a large board, or with a board where many of the members are not previously known by the chairman, or with an organisation where the environment within which it is working is changing.

All three of these conditions were in place when I took over as chairman of a quango in the South West of England, and I am very glad I called all its fourteen members. I was then able to chair my first meeting both well informed and with all members of the board feeling they had been consulted about the way forward from the outset.

Mentoring the CEO.

I have said mentoring rather than coaching, because in general CEO's will seek the advice that mentoring provides, rather than just the sounding board that some non-directive coaching offers. Nonetheless coaching and listening skills are vital in the relationship between the chairman and CEO, and the extent to which the chairman simply seeks to draw out the best from the CEO or on the other hand to recommend specific courses of action is one that each chairman must determine for himself. He must in the process of doing so be alive to the risks of prematurely killing off better ideas by recommending a good one.

I found that to support my quango CEO, I needed to hear her concerns at length once a week or more, and because she had far more experience of the operational environment in which she was working, much of the time I was seeking to draw her out rather than making prescriptive suggestions.

Protecting the organisation's reputation.

Whether he likes it or not, and however much he may feel it is an operational PR matter for the CEO and his PR agent or department to handle, the press and others will frequently look to the chairman. They will ask for views on the organisation, the industry in which it operates, and the effects of government policy on the organisation. They may well expect the chairman to make statements on the actions the organisation is taking in a crisis. So a chairman must make sure he is at all times up to speed with key operational questions.

On the plus side, it offers the chairman an opportunity to voice his opinions on relevant matters. I was once interviewed by a trade publication and took the opportunity to raise issues not of direct relevance to the operations of my organisation at that moment, but which helped to put the organisation in a good light, by showing that we were thinking more broadly about strategic issues.

Differences in the chairman's function depending on the size of the organisation

There is an epithet which can be useful in putting a limit to the roles that a chairman takes on, which those new chairmen unfamiliar with the role may find helpful. That is, to *only do what only the chairman can do*.

In a small voluntary organisation, for example, it is often the case that the chairman does a lot more than this. But it is useful to differentiate between those functions being carried out in the role of chairman and other tasks which are not part of that role. Many are simply being done because no-one else is there to do them, or because the chairman enjoys doing them.

A chairman of an arts charity of which I am a trustee enjoys putting together exhibitions of works that the charity owns, but he is aware that he is doing this outside of his role as chairman.

There is a danger of confusion where there is a CEO as well as a chairman who takes on additional functions. Any chairman so doing must put the relationship with the CEO ahead of the enjoyment he may get from doing other things within the organisation.

If there is any doubt, the chairman is well advised to give up any activities which might be construed as interference with the CEO's area of authority.

Chapter 4

DIGGING DEEPER INTO THE ORGANISATION

This is where particular sensitivity to the respective roles of the chairman and CEO is required. A chairman must know what is going on, and this may well require discussion with managers down the hierarchy – but without cutting across the CEO's authority.

Senior staff or managers should keep the chairman informed of their major projects and activities. They need to have their perspective on the organisation well understood at board level. Otherwise they risk being marginalised or worse. A good chairman will in any case familiarise himself with the activities of those reporting to the CEO, both in discussion with him and with the managers concerned.

A charity I worked with briefly had an excellent and experienced chairman who used to walk through the office, talking to staff members as he went. His benevolently paternal style enabled him to simultaneously be seen to care about each employee, and to get a more personal insight into the day to day working of the organisation.

I chose to adopt his approach when I became a chairman, and this became an important way for me to glean what was going on in the quango I chaired.

Committees

A common practice in larger organisations, and perhaps also in non-profits, is to set up sub-committees to deal with specific areas. A common example is finance. Often the CEO, finance director, company secretary, and possibly another non-executive director with relevant expertise will form a finance subcommittee. There are both advantages and potential pitfalls in doing this.

Advantages:

- There is often too much detail to be considered by the full board

- The area to be discussed may benefit from focussed expertise

- The time taken to discuss is inappropriate for the full board

- It may be useful for a smaller group to reach a tentative decision that can then be presented to the board for further discussion and approval.

Pitfalls:

• Particularly with finance there is a danger of the subcommittee becoming an "inner board" that takes decisions that are then rubber stamped by the full board without proper consideration

• The setting up of a subcommittee may be misused to avoid particular members of the full board having a say over a particular issue

Both these pitfalls can be avoided if the chairman has a seat on them. Alternatively he needs to be aware of the risks, and ensure that the composition of subcommittees does not encourage such behaviour.

Sensitive staff issues

Another area where a sub-committee may look into sensitive issues is staffing. Sometimes this might just be taken as "reserved business" for the non-executive members of the board, possibly together with the CEO. Executive directors and other staff who might normally be observers at a board meeting are often excluded. The way in which such exclusions are managed is sensitive , as there's a potential for a message to be read into who's being excluded.
The chairman must be aware of this. If the topic is likely to be difficult, the chairman should consider having reserved business as a permanent agenda item at which only board

members are present, with others invited in individually as necessary.

The chairman has a particular duty to make sure that none of the pitfalls are allowed to interfere with the proper powers of the full Board. In my view, the chairman should sit on any sub-committee that is considering key strategic issues, to ensure that this is the case.

CEO succession

Chairmen are often introduced into family-owned businesses where there is an issue with generational succession. An owner or managing partner may know and accept that he has to pass on the reins of power to a son, daughter, nephew or niece, but he may not have agreement over how and when this should occur. He has several options:

- Resign and walk away. Very few people in such a position are willing to do this, unless forced to for health or other personal reasons. It would usually be regarded by others as irresponsible unless or until a clear and competent successor is in place
- Appoint a successor in waiting and manage a gradual transition without external support. There may only be one natural successor, and this by default is what usually happens. There is a danger, however that the successor

will either slavishly follow the policies of his predecessor which may not be appropriate in changing times, or conversely, react against the style and substance of how things used to be done, without considering the changes with due care and consideration.

- Talk through the transitional process within the family, and thereby reach a consensus. The difficulty here is that disagreement may not be easy to resolve when many parties are attached to their opinions and the decision making process is not transparent and structured.

- Seek the advice of professional advisers. This only works to the extent that advisers are willing to risk controversy. An external accountant or lawyer is unlikely to be sufficiently assertive in resolving conflict, because it risks his relationship with the client.

- Appoint an external chairman. This is generally my preferred option. An independent chairman has both the responsibility and authority to see through the process, however difficult and lengthy it may be. He will also have the opportunity to bring out new ideas which could otherwise easily be lost in the discussion. There may for example be a case for changing the form of the business, for example from a partnership into a limited company, or even from a private to a public limited company. It is surprisingly common for very large family owned businesses, or public companies with large family holdings, to have serious succession issues. In the 1970's Tesco found itself in this situation, and was only resolved when Iain Maclaurin was appointed as Chief Executive. In such cases a high level of skill is required by a chairman to navigate the transition process.

Removal of a CEO

In extreme cases, the chairman may, with the agreement of the board, choose to dismiss the CEO. In theory this can occur in any type of organisation. It may be necessary to change the CEO without his agreement, on the grounds of chronic ill health for example. As in other cases of succession, a high level of sensitivity and skill is required by the chairman to carry the process through. Exceptionally careful listening to the views of all board members is essential.

Handling "difficult" board members

There will often be differences of opinion around a boardroom table. Usually these are minor, or easily manageable, and most directors are willing most of the time to accept the consensus view. If they are not, generally in my experience they resign.

Occasionally, however, a member will express a contrary view that either polarises the board or causes upset amongst other board members. It is important in such situations that the chairman does not immediately leap to the defence of the majority position. Every opportunity should be given to the dissenting member to have their say, and if necessary the chairman should meet with the dissenting member and others to resolve the issue outside the main board. Usually such dissent will have some validity that needs to be addressed, even if the final outcome is unchanged from the prevailing majority position.

Chapter 5

HOW A CHAIRMAN GETS AGREEMENT

Involving all board members

An incoming chairman typically has a brief period in which to establish himself with the existing members, before issues and events start to crowd in.

The best way for him to create trust is to phone each member of the board and sound them out on their perspective on the strengths, weaknesses, opportunities and threats to the organisation. This simultaneously achieves several useful outcomes -

- It allows the incoming chairman to get to know each director in a more relaxed way, away from the boardroom.
- It allows him to learn more about the organisation
- It gives him an insight into potential areas of conflict
- It also gives the existing members the opportunity to think through their ideas about the organisation in less confronting environment than many will find the board meetings to be.
- Recognise and accept differences. Each member will have their own perspective. Generally, if they feel heard, they will accept the consensus view.
- Focus on difficult issues. Once the trust of the members has been earned by actively listening and acknowledging their views, difficult issues can be faced up to.

A charity whose board I sat on had a chronic financial problem arising from reductions in government support for its activities. Because the chairman had a good relationship with each of the trustees, it was possible to make difficult and confronting decisions relating to staff and property, while retaining the good will of some of the older members of the board who had been there for over ten years.

Similarly, a quango I chaired had reduced levels of public sector income, and needed to transform into a Community Interest Company. In order to do this effectively, many board members needed to stand down, and the existing chief executive need to join the board. This was contentious, but the process was a smooth one because of the relationships I had established with each board member.

Involve all members of the board

There is a temptation for some chairmen to attempt to marginalise or inhibit contributions from those board members who have a habit of dissenting or appearing to make difficulties for the rest of the board. In my experience this is not a good idea. The likely outcome of resisting contrary views is to entrench the member in his view, and even to polarise the board. Frequently the contrary view being voiced is shared to some extent by others round the table but have not had the courage to speak out. There will also often be some validity in the contrary view. The open airing of these issues is nearly always the best way forward!

Recognise and accept differences

Boards may split down the middle on certain issues, and it is important to accept this. If agreement cannot be reached in discussion, it is often appropriate to go to a vote. This generally clears the air, and allows members to move on to the next issue under consideration.

Focussing on a difficult issue

Because they may be closer to or better informed on an issue, the chairman and CEO may well reach a view not currently shared by other directors. It may take time to reach a consensus and there are several strategies to do this. Setting up a sub-group which includes leading proponents of both sides of an argument can be helpful. In extreme cases, a chairman may seek to recruit more expertise on to the board in a certain area in order to help resolve an issue. He must be careful that he is not doing this in order to "pack" the board with like- minded individuals to outweigh the pre-existing members.

An example of this in the Market and Coastal Towns process occurred when I chaired a town group, where the local business community was at loggerheads with the elected Town Council over the direction the process should take. Although I was present as a member of the business community, I took the view that inclusion of others was paramount in having the process work, and those business owners who didn't like it would have to put up with the consensus. We produced a plan with forty eight projects, some very demanding. About two thirds of them were adopted in one form or another. There were a couple of occasions where I had to take decisions to a vote, but all in all I think the process helped to create additional community cohesion, and subsequently the town has developed some useful community assets, including a Transition group, a prizewinning Farmers' Market, and is now in the process of creating a community owned bookshop.

Chapter 6

HOW TO FIND A CHAIRMAN

Who chooses?

Although it is vital that the CEO has a say, and the relationship between him and the chairman is pivotal, technically the board will choose its chairman. They can choose one from within their ranks , or find an outsider. This raises several options.

An existing independent Director.

In charities and other not for profit organisations, this is usually the source of the chairman. If the board is unpaid, it is unlikely that an outsider will -from a standing start - have the knowledge and commitment required to step into the role. So if there is a director or trustee who is ready, willing and able to take on the job, why not?

In a commercial business, it does happen but is less common. Occasionally there is an independent director with specific skill and experience that qualifies him to do the job. However, the focus on ability is naturally more intense when profits are at stake, and the board will frequently look elsewhere.

The Ex CEO

It is very common for the retiring CEO to become chairman, and on the face of it there are advantages:

- He knows the business well - probably better than anyone else
- He knows all the board members and has experience working with them
- He knows the issues that the new CEO will be faced with

However, there are also drawbacks:

- His mindset is that of a CEO and he is likely to be tempted to interfere excessively with the work of the new CEO
- He has a strong predetermined view of how things should go, and is likely to project this, consciously or unconsciously.

- He may or may not have the ability to stand back and allow the board to explore ideas freely, and to refine strategy over time.

I must own up to presiding over a process in which my successor as chairman of a quango was the chief executive. As it happens she was in my view well suited to the job, and in that case the advantages outweighed any possible drawbacks.

Acquaintances of the CEO or outgoing chairman

This is another frequently used option. It smacks of cronyism or the old boys network, but in a small industry or locality, it is often the case that the best available candidate is already known to the board. It is particularly important that candidates known to the board are rigorously selected, and the use of an external selection professional can help to ensure that this is being done and is seen to be done.

Executive Search

This is the path pursued by those concerned with possible retrospective criticism, and will involve advertising, the use of an external consultant, and systematic HR procedures. Often, even after this process, you will end up with one of the above candidate categories. I have been selected in this way, to a board where I already knew the existing CEO, the acting chairman, his predecessor, and several other board members. Executive search is no guarantee of avoiding a previously known candidate from becoming the chairman.

Chapter 7

HOW TO INTRODUCE THE NEW CHAIRMAN INTO THE ORGANISATION

The new chairman has a responsibility to establish himself and his key relationships in the organisation as quickly as possible. Equally, the organisation, and primarily the CEO has a duty to facilitate this process.

Make sure the chairman has contact details for all board members.

Obvious perhaps, but it is by no means universally observed. Ideally the chairman should have all board members landline, mobile and email details. Only he can make the calls, but it can be made easier for him to do it.

Issue a press release

The relevant local or sector press at the very least should be informed of the appointment. Almost invariably, one or more will want to print an article, and often an interview with the chairman. I have found this to be an invaluable opportunity to say more about my wider views of the relevant industry, its opportunities and threats, and generally to be better known and understood.

Inform key stakeholders

Important customers, investors, suppliers, even competitors, will want to know about the new chairman and what his view of the future is for the organisation. The press release can be used to inform these, possibly with a covering letter from the CEO depending on the nature of his relationship with them.

Senior Managers

It will be important for the incoming chairman to establish a relationship with key senior managers. However it is unlikely to be a matter of urgency. It is up to the chairman to determine the level of contact he has with staff below board level. There is an art to doing so in a way that does not cut across the authority of the CEO.

Chapter 8

HOW CAN AN ORGANISATION AFFORD A CHAIRMAN?

A chairman must justify any costs he incurs.

In a very small organisation, albeit one that wants to grow, the chairman should be seen as an investment with a return in line with other investment decisions. It would be reasonable, for example, to expect, in addition to fulfilling his statutory roles, chairing meetings etc. that the value of his input exceeds his costs within two years. This is of course very difficult to quantify. A business is not a scientific experiment, and there will be other variables that simultaneously affect its profitability.

In a small business, his value as a coach and mentor to the CEO has a market price, say £200/hour. On this basis, if he spends two hours per week solely on focussed conversations with the CEO, his market value for this service alone might be £20,000 per year.

At the other end of the spectrum is the view that the chairman can be seen as responsible for the overall performance of the business. He can therefore be judged – and rewarded - in relationship to any increase in value of the business. This is relatively easy to achieve in a listed company with a quoted share price, and is often done by the issue of stock options, which give a direct reward as a result of share price increases.

One might rephrase the original question –how can a business afford not to have a chairman? – many of the roles described in this book are essential to a business and if there is no chairman they will often need to be performed by the chief executive, who as we have seen is often not endowed with the time, ability or inclination to carry them out.

Strategic decisions are likely to be cumulative in effect – that means that the benefits of making them are long lasting. If a chairman causes the business to make a decision that saves his annual salary each year, then he will be worth more each year for example:

Year	1	2	3	4
Salary	20,000	20,000	20,000	20,000
Annual benefit	20,000	40,000	60,000	80,000
Net annual benefit	0	20,000	40,000	60,000
Cumulative net benefit	0	20,000	60,000	120,000

In non-profit organisations, chairmen are often not paid at all, and this can be seen as appropriate if he is not expected to bring any financial benefit to the organisation. Frequently, however, non-profit organisations are under threat of closure if losses are not controlled, and a good chairman can make the difference between survival or failure. In such situations, is it appropriate to pay the chairman? Perhaps it should be considered more often.

In some public sector organisations, such as health authorities, the burden of responsibility , the size of the organisation, and the risk of negative publicity is such that it would be difficult indeed to find an effective chairman without paying them sometimes substantial amounts.

So there are wide range of situations , but the general message is that there is an appropriate amount and mechanism to reward chairman in each case. There is certainly no affordability excuse to rule out having a chairman in any business which has aspirations to grow, even if only modestly.

The limitation may ultimately be on the number of individuals ready willing and able to fulfil the role!

Chapter 9

CHOOSING OTHER BOARD MEMBERS

Who else should be on the board? The answer -or answers-
to this question are surprisingly varied, depending on the
type of organisation and the business culture in which it
operates. I have sat on the board of a commercial business
where only shareholders were represented, and the
operational manager did not have a seat. Many farming co-
operatives adopt this model, where the purpose of the board
is seen to be to control the activities of the manager, who is
seen as inferior to the board in the organisational hierarchy.

In most small commercial companies , the operational manager is also a shareholder, often the sole proprietor, and it would be curious if in this situation he did not have a seat on the board. But it is not a necessary requirement.

A quango I chaired was initially run with the Executive Director not on the board. Several of the directors felt that when government support started to fall away, it was appropriate for her to become a director, but the issue was contentious.

What other operational directors should sit on the board? I believe that any manager who heads a department and has an insight into the strategic direction of the business should have a seat. Those departments likely to have such an insight, in approximate order of relevance would be finance, marketing, production, HR.

A key requirement of an operational director is that he understands the distinction between his management and directorial responsibilities. He is not on the board to fight his corner in the organisation, he is there to participate in the proper functioning of the board in determining the strategic course of the business.

What about non-executives (NED's)? In some entities, for example Community Interest Companies, it is a requirement that NED's outnumber executive directors. This is to ensure that any conflict of interest is decided in favour of the business, whose profits or surplus must be used for the benefit of the community defined in its articles of association, not the employees or operational directors.

Creating a matrix of experience and skills of the existing board can be a useful way to determine what is missing , and these attributes can be used to form the basis of a man spec in recruiting a new non-exec.

Here is a list of attributes we drew up in South West Food and Drink as desirable to be represented on the board:

- Strategic/ Public Funding
- Farming/ Growing
- Drinks (i.e. has experience of the drink industry!)
- Manufacturing
- Processing
- Skills/Training
- Research/Consultant
- PR
- Finance

- Consumer Facing
- Tourism
- Organic
- Distribution/ Supply Chain
- Environmental
- EU
- Sales & Marketing

In practice we subdivided these categories, in order to clarify the skills of the existing 14 non-exec board members.

I suggest that most small organisations will not need to go to such lengths, and will be more concerned with those people who can demonstrate that they have contributed to the profitability of businesses in their earlier careers.

It is also important that anyone recruited to the board understands and is capable of enacting the distinction between a director and a manager. This can be difficult for some hands-on business owners without previous board experience.

Chapter 10

YOUR NEXT STEP IN FINDING A CHAIRMAN

You may or may not be certain yet that you want a chairman.

But you strongly suspect that it is worth starting the process to find one. What do you do?

Consult with your professional advisers.

Every solicitor and accountant I have spoken to says that good governance lags growth in businesses, or to put it another way, most organisations would be more effective in the longer term if they took steps earlier to develop their boards. Your solicitor and accountant see hundreds of organisations and will have formed their own opinions on what to do at any stage of development. You may not agree with what they have to say, but they will have a valuable perspective that is worth hearing.

Don't go to an executive search agency –yet.

I do not recommend this until you are very clear what you are looking for and why. Executive search agencies are expensive, and highly motivated to place someone whether or not you have fully though through what you want. They will encourage you to go through the "Job spec, man spec" process, but there is a prior stage in the process.

Strategise!

OK, so you think your new chairman will do this for you when he arrives. It is true that he will, but the more thought you have already given to it, the better able you will be to assess a candidate chairman's suitability, and the better use you will be able to make of him - even if it is only a paragraph on where you are now and another on where you want to be in five years' time.

Consider appointing an interim chairman.

In order to go through an initial strategizing process, you could appoint an interim chairman who specialises in doing this. He may be a consultant, or the chairman of another organisation. He may even be a potential permanent chairman, but you will need at this stage to have the freedom to use him for a fixed period of say three months. As the chairman, he will have a greater level of commitment to the organisation than someone hired simply as a freelance consultant.

You should expect him to

- Take you through a strengths, weaknesses opportunities and threats(SWOT) process for the business
- To develop a draft or outline strategy
- To develop a governance plan

- And only then to define the characteristics of a permanent chairman

He would probably need to meet with you and any other board members about six times over the course of his chairmanship, and to spend about a week, depending on the complexity of the business, spread over the three months, producing his assessment and recommendations.

In the course of that time, there may well be events that require board decisions, and you will be able to experience working with a chairman to develop the business in real time.

Chapter 11

HOW A CHAIRMAN MANAGES MEETINGS

Many people think that the main job of a chairman is to manage meetings. I hope that the contents of this guide have amply illustrated that there are many functions of a chairman, and that managing meetings is only one of many skills required.

Having said that, the board meeting is the prime public space in which the chairman is seen to operate, and by which he is likely to be judged in the first instance.

At the risk of repetition-

- The chairman's job is to create a safe space in which constructive inputs from other board members can occur, and from which consensus or majority decisions can be made. All other rules are subservient to this end.
- The chairman is responsible for the integrity of the space . This requires that
    - o Meetings are held in a location conducive to effective working
    - o Meetings start at the appointed time
    - o Meetings finish by the appointed time
    - o An agenda is circulated with any relevant papers, generally at least a week before to allow time to read them.
    - o The agenda should have the time date and place of the meeting, apologies for absence, approval of the arising from the minutes of

the previous meeting, and then other items for discussion. The final items should be any other business and time, date and place of the next meeting.

o For regular board meetings, the times are often decided a year in advance, so that they can be diarised by all board members. Otherwise there is a risk of a lengthy process of determining a convenient time for the next meeting after every meeting.
With large boards, it is generally futile to attempt to get 100% attendance at every meeting.

o Appropriate minutes are taken and circulated

Here is an Agenda of the Devon Towns Forum which I chaired. In some respects it was easy to chair, because most of the members were chairmen of town community groups. However there was a risk of meetings running over two hours, which I regarded as the maximum useful length. Hence the inclusion of a finish time and note to remind members of it. In order for this approach to work, the chairman must take firm control from the outset of each item. Far more can be covered in this way.

Market and Coastal Towns Association

The Devon Towns Forum

Devon County Council

Meeting of the DTF Management Board: 7.00pm to 9.00pm Tuesday 3rd Oct 2006

Venue: The Coaver Club, County Hall, Exeter.

AGENDA

1) Apologies
2) Previous Meeting (AGM 11-July-2006) and Annual Report 2006
3) Matters arising from the above and welcome to new members Jane Mills and Vernon Whitlock also Bob Buxton elected as Vice Chairman.
4) MCTA SWAN BDOR report 'An Exciting future for Community Plans'. (see notes)
5) DTF support for Joint Partnership Working (see notes)
6) DTF Sponsored Devon Renaissance Funding Master Classes, PD (see notes)
7) Next Area for DR Funding Master Class?
8) DTF support for Bridges Event for North Devon and Torridge up-date CW, JM & PD (see notes)
9) DTF representation & feedback: (the DTF are represented on the following groups)
    - DCC Housing Appraisal Steering Group BB
    - DRN Management Board TLD, DRN STAG, PD
    - DCC Project Database Steering Group TLD, CW, PD
    - NASP and Common Ground PD, CM & TLD
    - Devon Renaissance, TLD, PD
10) DTF Sponsored CIB Funding Advisor Training. Feedback from Jane Mills
11) DTF sponsored SWCO Website Refresher Workshop 6th Oct 2006
12) MCTA Annual Conference 2&3rd Feb 2007 details and invitations to be announced
13) Budget up-date PD
14) Future DTF Events
15) Any other urgent business
16) Dates and Venue for future Board Meetings

Please note the Chairman has asked that the meeting begin promptly and conclude not later than 9.00pm.

- Before the meeting, ask yourself if you have any unresolved issues with any of the board members that might affect the running of the meeting. If possible resolve them before the meeting. For example, if you had promised to send a piece of information to someone, had you done it, or had you been sure that the person had received it? This will reduce the scope for any resentment which could undermine the smooth running of the meeting.

- For each item, invite the person leading on it, often but not always the CEO, to introduce the subject and report. Then open the subject up for discussion.
- Do not allow vociferous members of the board to dominate the discussion, particularly if this is preventing quieter members from contributing
- There is an art to deciding the extent to which you voice your own views. Your primary job is to elicit the views of others, and not to manipulate the discussion so that it goes your way.
- In practice the views of the chairman and CEO will usually prevail because on most issues they will be better informed – but this is not an excuse to gloss over the expression of alternative opinions.
- Very occasionally, agreement is not possible around the table, and a vote must be called. The terms of the voting will be in the articles of association. In my experience it is better if the chairman does not vote, unless a casting vote is required. I have been required to place a casting

vote on two occasions, and because due process was scrupulously observed, there was a willingness of all members to support the final outcome.

Chapter 12

CHAIRING PUBLIC SECTOR FUNDED COMMUNITY ORGANISATIONS

I have chaired several different types of public sector funded organisations, and here are a few examples.

South West Market and Coastal Towns initiative.

The key to chairing this organisation was to accept and simultaneously work to resolve a number of cultural differences. These existed both within and outside the group.

Within it, there were conflicts between private and local business members, and elected representatives from the many layers of local government (Parish, Town, District and County).Outside it, between the community as a whole and the Regional Development Agency, which had a civil service culture moderated by newly recruited staff with some business experience. Some people within the community found the process infuriatingly slow or even opaque, particularly those from a small business or military background, where action was more highly prized than consideration. Others were politically suspicious, particularly if they were UKIP or Conservative, and therefore overtly against initiatives of the then Labour Government, which the Regional Development Agency was.

We took the view that we should be as ambitious as possible in the projects we included in our Plan, and ended up with 48 projects, of which two thirds were progressed.

Arising from the twenty or so towns in Devon in the MCTI process, we formed an umbrella group, the Devon Towns Forum. The purpose of this was to facilitate towns supporting each other through the process, and as we had been an early completer of a plan, I also became chairman of the county group.

Partly because of what I had already learned, and partly because of the more co-operatively motivated fellow chairmen on this group, it was in many ways an easier group to lead. Frustrations with the RDA continued to be a feature, but I had already factored this in to my interpretation of the process.

The top level Regional grouping in the process was the South West Market and Coastal Towns Network, which included the chairs of the county groups, and worked with the RDA to refine and develop the process. I became the first chairman, and we continued to operate until the process as a whole completed.

My conclusion on the value of the process is that it raised the level of community led activity throughout the rural south west, and involved many hundreds of people, some of whom, like me, had not previously participated in local politics. It required a considerable input of time, which personally I was happy to give, as it provided me with the opportunity to learn about many things.

In retrospect it was a great privilege to play a leading role in such an ambitious initiative, and to see so many projects come to fruition, even if at the time progress seemed slow.

Chapter 13

CHAIRING PUBLIC SECTOR FUNDED INDUSTRIAL SECTOR ORGANISATIONS

South West Food and Drink

In 2009, it was suggested that I apply for the chairmanship of South West Food and Drink. Almost immediately after I took up the position, the then Labour government cut funding progressively. The general election of 2010 brought in the Conservative and Liberal Democrat Coalition, and the new government did away with the RDA, and the core funding it provided to the organisation. Over the next two years, we shed costs and converted from a quango into a Community Interest Company (CIC) which continues successfully to offer services to those who are still willing to pay for strategically motivated initiatives in the food and drink industry.

One key decision we made was to appoint the Chief Executive to the Board, which was perhaps surprisingly contentious. I have noticed that there is a tendency in rural England to have boards consisting entirely of non-executives with managers reporting to them, even in some commercial businesses. It seems to me that at least one manager needs to have a board position in order to keep an effective relationship between the board and the managers and other staff.

Chapter 14

CHAIRING PUBLIC SECTOR FUNDED CHARITIES

I have experienced two types of such organisations:

(i)   Local Authority funded
Torbay Coast and Countryside Trust, for which I
worked as a sustainable projects consultant, had
a staff and chief executive with broadly public
sector and charity backgrounds, and a strong and
widely drawn board of trustees, many of whom
had substantial commercial experience. The
chairman at the time I arrived, who I had
previously known, was a distinguished retired
land agent, very familiar with the financial
constraints on land based organisations.
The organisation was described as unique by the
chief executive, but in my view bore some
resemblance to the National Trust in its
aspirations and activities. Its main funder was
Torbay Council, a unitary authority formed in
1999. The vision and vigour of the chief
executive, combined with the professionalism
and experience of the chairman and board, and
the need of Torbay Council for imaginative

management of extensive land holdings and related buildings, created a superb environment for a wide range of environmentally sustainable projects and activities.

(ii)   Arts Council funded
Beaford Arts is a North Devon based charity of which I became a trustee in 2012, at the request of the chairman. Severe reductions in funding required difficult decisions to be made, and I and another trustee were recruited largely because of our commercial experience, to participate in a carefully considered process of rationalisation. The existing trustees were remarkably tolerant of our blunt expressions of how we saw things, and we reached a remarkable level of consensus on the way forward in no small part thanks to an excellent chairman.

Chapter 15

CHAIRING JOINT MARKETING ENTITIES

In the late eighties I was invited on to the board of
Peninsular Pigs Ltd, a breeding and marketing company
of which Quickes, for which I was Commercial Director,
was the largest, but still a minority, shareholder.
The company had been started to breed and "multiply"
a new strain of pigs .
Quickes had the nucleus herd from which breeding stock
went to second and third generation multipliers, and
then on to final producers.
I now realise that the essence of chairing this company
was to resolve the different interests of Quickes, and the
other shareholders who were keen to avoid incurring
any costs. Unfortunately the chairman was one of those
other shareholders and was therefore in a difficult
conflict of interest position.
We eventually decided with my strong approval to sell
the company to a much larger breeder, which we did at
an advantageous price.

Also while at Quickes, I set up a joint export marketing
company Alliance des Fromages Anglais, (AFA) which
still exists, to sell farmhouse cheddar and traditionally

made stilton to France and other parts of continental Europe.

This business, of which I was the first chairman, has now grown to a turnover of over £5 million.

The key to the success of this operation was to manage the cultural differences, most obviously between the French agent and customer base and the English suppliers. Because I had been managing the French agent for the previous three years, I had a relatively good understanding of this. Perhaps more challenging was managing the expectations of the three suppliers. Although they were from the same industry, they were very different in size and ownership structure. Clawson Stilton was a farmer owned co-operative, with substantial exporting experience. Wyke Farms was a very large block cheddar producer, albeit from farming roots, and still owned by the Clothier family. Quickes was a much smaller farm based artisan cheesemaker. Strategically the company was a great success, paving the way for substantially increased market penetration of high quality English cheese into the French market.

CONCLUSION

In the course of writing this guide, I have reconnected with some core insights arising from my experiences on the boards of the wide range of organisations I have been privileged to serve.
Here are some of them:

- There is no substitute for an effective chief executive.
- A good chief executive will seek support from wherever he can get it.
- A good chairman can do more than most to ensure that he gets it
- Conflict resolution is an art that repays preparation and experience
- Dissent can be productive if properly managed
- Organisations are there to serve all their stakeholders
- It is the duty of the chairman to ensure that the pleasure and profit from his organisation's activities outweigh the effort and trouble that go to produce them.
- Aim to have fun doing it!

www.ingramcontent.com/pod-product-compliance
Lightning Source LLC
Chambersburg PA
CBHW070942180526
45168CB00003B/1141